ONE TRUTH! JESUS CHRIST

Volume II Of The N.E.M. Discipleship Formation Series

Dcn. Ralph Poyo

AUTHORS NOTE

New Evangelization Ministries is dedicated to training saints to lead hearts to Christ. This mission is not a program, but a one-on-one process where a current disciple leads an individual to Jesus and then trains them up to become a mature Disciple of Jesus Christ.

This booklet is the second in the NEM Discipleship Formation Series. Each booklet is a tool for disciples to use in their training of new followers of Christ. We believe this one-on-one process must be the work of individuals, not programs. The sheer nature of the disciple is self-replicating and, for this reason, each disciple must learn how to be one and train others to follow.

Keep checking our website for releases of new tools.
www.NewEvangelizationMinistries.org

TABLE OF CONTENTS

ACKNOWLEDGEMENTS

Special thanks to my wife and editor, Susan. It was through your love of Jesus that I came to know him intimately. You challenged me to believe and to grow into a man of God who could lead his family. Even now, you provide me with feedback and inspiration to move farther out in faith and to love more fearlessly.

Thank you for all your editorial efforts with this project and being the initial disciple to show me the way.

INTRODUCTION

One of the greatest deficiencies in parish life today is in our modeling of what a disciple of Jesus really is. Many who are a part of current generations understand a disciple to simply be membership in a parish and attendance at Mass. Beyond that, they have little understanding of discipleship. While we could take many pages to unpack adequately and define this term, the brevity of this booklet demands that we provide a concise view and definition.

With each chapter, we have provided reference numbers to the Catechism of the Catholic Church. We believe that this resource is a gift from the Holy Spirit for the Church in the Twenty-First Century. Our hope is that Disciples will lead their students into this resource and teach them how to use it as they use this tool.

Followers

It is important to note that being a Disciple of Jesus Christ is not just being a student of a set of teachings (Scriptures & Church Documents) from someone in the past. It is not like being a disciple of the teachings of Buda. Our faith is built on the premise that our God is a living God, an entity in the present moment. As such, a disciple's first role is to **follow** Jesus. If we don't literally follow him, we are not living by the truth He teaches! Upon encountering The Lord, we make a decision to give him our heart and establish a relationship. Like any other relationship, growing with Jesus requires time, communication, further encounters, and trust, in order that love may flow between us. All of these require **being with him - following him.** Therefore, once a person encounters Jesus, he or she makes it their aim to remain with Him for the rest of eternity. They want to grow closer to Him and never leave Him.

This sounds confusing because there is not a physical person for us to follow. We are accustomed to having someone present to guide us. Like going on a tour at a national monument, there is a particular person who identifies himself or herself as the leader and they guide us around the monument, educating us on the history and elements of the monument. How can we follow Jesus, if he isn't here? Or is he?

The truth we come to understand is that Jesus is truly present in the form of the Holy Spirit. This was the great epiphany of the Apostles at the Feast of Pentecost. Jesus promised to be with them for the rest of time. He was referring to the coming of the Holy Spirit. Since the Spirit and He are one (Mystery of the Trinity), Jesus is also present. In the Spirit's presence, the Apostles began to experience life in the spiritual realm. We consist of spirit and flesh but lost our understanding of the spiritual life with original sin. Therefore, we were born into our earthly life only aware of our physical existence. Being "born from above" or "born again" (John 3:3), as Jesus told Nicodemus, is the birth of new life where we are given the Holy Spirit and now have the capacity to live spiritually as well as physically. Remember, Jesus came to bring us home and that home is Heaven and a new earth. So we must learn how to live in the Spirit (spiritually) in preparation for our journey home.

Learning how to follow Jesus requires learning how to make Jesus present in our every moment. The fundamental disciplines listed in the book of Acts (2:42) are examples of how we come in contact with The Lord in specific ways. As we exercise these activities, we are making the effort to be present to Jesus, by engaging the Holy Spirit, who in turn, instructs us in the truth. To live the truth of the Gospels is to proclaim, by the way you live your life that you are choosing to live in the Kingdom of God. This truth requires an intentional pulling away from the world. This process is a struggle because it means we must live differently, no longer according to norms and passions of the world, but by the will of Christ as instructed by the Holy Spirit.

A disciple of Jesus Christ is a follower who makes it his first priority to **remain with Jesus** for the rest of eternity. For us to do this, we must learn through our discipleship training and instruction from the Holy Spirit how to live in the Spirit while existing on earth. When we fail to do so, we must reconcile quickly and continue the relationship. Having the true model of discipleship is critical to maintaining a healthy body of Christ. When the model becomes defiled with false witness and teaching, those who follow, grow into something quite different. Therefore, **it is critical that every new disciple become diligent in their effort to learn from and instruct future disciples in union with mother Church**. She has been given the task of holding true the deposit of faith.

After the saving work of Christ on Earth, the Father sent the Holy Spirit to establish the Church and then work through the Church to bring believers home. This initiated the next phase of the saving plan of God. Humanity would now be able to attain the life of God (Heaven) through an intimate relationship with the Holy Spirit. The only way this plan can work is if those who believe in Jesus remain faithful to him in loving humility. Jesus placed a great trust in his apostles when he passed on to them his mission. He trusted them to hold on to the deposit of faith given to them and pass it on to subsequent generations. Therefore, every generation of disciples is charged with this same mission and carries the same responsibility to remain faithful to what Jesus gave us.

This means that to profess in your heart to be a follower of Christ is to embrace and adhere to **all** of his teachings. It is not acceptable for any disciple of Christ to add to nor take away from the teachings he has given the Church. To become a member of the Church is to be completely faithful to **all** his teachings. We live in a time where many are picking and choosing which teachings they will adhere to. In doing this, they are not living the truth nor are they living in faith. They have begun to live their own new religion based on whatever is convenient to them in the moment.

Our Responsibility

When we profess our belief in Christ and receive Baptism, we are professing our intention to join the apostles in the faith of Jesus Christ and the teachings of His Church. This means that we have a duty to learn the Church's teachings so that we are capable of leading others to Christ and training them up in the truth.

In one sense, the Lord places a sacred trust in every disciple who desires to follow him. He looks to them to make sure that what they share with others is nothing less than that with which the Church whole-heartedly believes. While it is true that the Holy Spirit has been given to us to teach us this truth, we must also remember that Jesus gave us the Church to guard and protect the truth.

The Holy Spirit has been guarding and protecting the Church and it's deposit of truth from the beginning. This reality is something we can have tremendous faith and assurance in. Therefore, as we move forward in your discipleship training, always remember that you should check what you are learning and interpreting in light of what the Church definitively teaches on that subject. The Holy Spirit has given us a tremendous gift in the Catechism of the Catholic Church (CCC). This document contains a clear explanation of what the Church believes and is extremely useful for instructing others.

Having clearly defined the responsibility of what we must learn and pass on to others, let us begin to focus in on four critical elements of this Church you have joined.

THE CHURCH IS ONE

(CCC 811-822)

While every member of the Church has their own relationship with God and their own path to the Beatific Vision, that path also unites us as one body. St. Paul writes about this in his first letter to the Corinthians (12:12-31). He articulates how although we are many, we are meant to be one body -- His body. I believe this is a teaching that, while mentioned often in our churches, is not lived out as it should be.

The image of a body is powerful and effective. St. Paul speaks of the many parts and purposes of the body and yet the body is united in one life form. It is our sinfulness that seeks to remain separated from the body, from other believers. Our pride, selfishness, and self-centeredness keep us comfortably away from everyone else.

Let me explain, it is shame and fear that keep us distant from each other as the fear of what may be revealed about who we really are and how bad we really struggle becomes a reality. Shame has a way of measuring and comparing. Yet, comparison does not belong in Christ! It is a tool used by the devil to separate us from each other. Why? To keep us divided! Why? So we don't achieve what Christ has come to do -- Unite us with his Father!

It is our sinfulness that drives a wedge in the whole body or community of believers. We rely not on God for our provision but on our own abilities. Relying on ourselves, not trusting in God, creates a chasm that distances ourselves from others as a defense. In my travels around the country, the communities where the Spirit of The Lord has been most powerful have been those who were able to share openly and honestly about their lives. In these communities, individuals were able to talk about their struggles and support one another as a community. Trusting one another and helping each part of the body of Christ prompted great growth in faith.

Choosing Christ is to choose his Church. To desire to be unified with Christ in an intimate relationship with him, is to become united with other disciples. Often times we control our growth in God by dictating who we will come close to. We would prefer to remain comfortably aloof and ambiguous so that others can't really learn too much about us. We come up with excuses for why we can't join this group or go on that retreat when the real reason is that we fear the light that exposes what we try desperately to hide.

Those who grow in authentic faith find in these small groups opportunities to be challenged and stretched as they are coaxed out of their comfort zones and into the unknown where Christ is in charge. Faith can't be just learning more about God, it has to include trusting him with all our lives.

So Christ calls us out of our own fears and into his body where we all have different gifts and all play different roles but are equal in His sight. With Jesus, we are all equal; equally loved, equally wanted, and equally purposed. This is the body of Christ.

Practical Application
If we are going to draw closer to Christ, he wants us to draw closer to others on the journey. This will require us to re-orient our way of thinking and living to make this an honest attempt. Pursuing God can't be just a personal adventure. We are called to give away what we have received. Therefore, we are going to have to work at sharing our lives with others. Those who learn this lesson will tell you that their greatest fruits came from sharing the difficult situations with others. That is where the power is!

As a Father, I must lead my family into the body of Christ. However, it is no longer acceptable for me to look to just the needs of my immediate family. If what I profess is true then I must also look to the needs of my new family - the family of God. While Satan would have me serve false gods of this world, perhaps by engaging in activities that draw me away from Christ's plan for my day, I must remember to "keep my eyes fixed on Jesus, the author and perfector of my faith" (Hebrews 12:2). I must see that there are important activities to invest my time in and the time of my family. Drawing closer to Christ requires that I look at life through His eyes, seeing the purpose He has for my life and growth as a part of the body. As a community then, we must regain our identity as Children of God and help our families to do so as well.

While working as a Youth Minister, I used to bring my daughters with me to the places in our city where the homeless lived. We ministered to the poor in our community by handing out sandwiches we had made. While it was sometimes frightening to visit such poverty, it was important to minister to these individuals, members of the body of Christ, as we felt called to. How encouraging, too, to witness how my kids looked forward to giving up a major part of their Saturday to feed the homeless. This is just one example of an activity we may be called to do to build up His kingdom here on earth. We must keep our eyes open to these opportunities for growth or we may just miss them. What kind of outreach intimidates you? Ask the Spirit to go with you and friend.

THE CHURCH IS HOLY

(CCC 823-829)

Throughout the ages, ever since Adam and Eve sinned, there has been a call back to holiness. Every Disciple of Jesus Christ is called to enter the battle for holiness. The Church, while filled with sinners, is still holy because God makes it so. It is only when we try to be holy of our own ability and strength, do we fall short for only in union with the Holy Spirit can we achieve the self control needed to obey.

In this battle for holiness, many of us misunderstand the fight that is required. We are tempted to rise up, bolstered by our own will power and not sin. This is a deceptive trap laid by the devil to keep us bound to sin. The truth is that we can't attain holiness apart from God.

St. Paul, in his letter to the Romans (3:20), clearly says that no one will be justified by following the Law. Justification means that Christ declares us righteous. It would more accurately be said this way; Christ will not declare anyone righteous by their attempt to live by the Law. Why? Because no one can live by the Ten Commandments on their own strength. Each of us lacks something and someone that would enable us to do that.

"Well Deacon Ralph, if we can't live by the Ten Commandments, then why did God give them to us?" Paul reveals the answer to us in the second half of verse twenty. The purpose of the Law is to reveal sin. God gives us the Law as a light to see the fact that even with our very best effort, we all fall short and cannot live perfectly.

Like a student struggling with a difficult math problem turns to their teacher for help, God desires that we recognize the difficulty of living as we should and ask for help. God uses the Law to call us back to repentance and humility. Many of us choose to take the route we are tempted with, the route of avoiding real relationship and simply trying to attain holiness (and salvation) through our own efforts at living a "good" life.

If you remember your religious instruction about the state of our souls when we were born, you will recall that we were born with "Original ___." Every person born into the world was lacking the

"Sanctifying _____" that enabled us to live holy lives. Sanctify means to "make holy" and grace can be defined as "sharing in the life of God." Therefore, lacking sanctifying grace is to lack the life of God that enables us to live holiness.

So, as the Holy Spirit was sent to the Church on the feast of Pentecost (Acts Chapter 2), He was also sent to each member of the Church. It has been and will ultimately be the work of the Holy Spirit to make the Church One, Holy, Catholic, and Apostolic. It is the work of God to make us holy. "If that is true, Deacon, then what are we supposed to do?"

Practical Application

We are called to enter into a relationship of deep love with God. The entire goal is to get to heaven and the process for that union begins, hopefully, on earth. Through faith in Christ's redemptive work, we have the opportunity to begin that union through the Holy Spirit. It is in this relationship where we grow in love with God.

Let us remember our initial conversion to Christ? Was it not a response of gratitude and love for Jesus who died on the cross for us? Once we embraced that belief, that Jesus really died for us, our faith led us to humbly accept our sinful state. We are sinners and in desperate need of a savior. When we accepted Jesus, we opened the door to receive the gift of the Holy Spirit and begin our journey to union with God.

That union doesn't happen instantly upon our death but over a period of time. Our life with God begins anew in the Spirit who enables us to grow in faith, hope and love in God. So as we start our spiritual disciplines, we must also respond to the truth we are learning about. This should be a very practical process of ongoing conversion.

For example, we should always ask for the help of the Holy Spirit to guide us in our journey. He knows where the best place is to start. So imagine that he wants to help us and lead us to read the passage "You shall not lie". Once he magnifies that teaching in our minds, we must then ask again for the help to live it.

This begins the process of learning how to die to ourselves. Once we commit to living out the truth of this process, the battle begins as the Spirit puts us in situations where we must tell the truth. Where, in self love, we once lied to shield ourselves from possible rejection or trouble, we now, out of love for Jesus, seek to honor and please him by telling the truth.

To seek to become holy is to seek to live out the Theological and Corporal Virtues. They are not easy to live out because of our fallen nature, but with the Holy Spirit, we can gain the motivation (through love) to fight and the grace to live in the truth. Go find and study the Theological and Corporal Virtues, then practice living them.

THE CHURCH IS CATHOLIC

CCC 830-856

These days, the term "Catholic Church" is popularly understood to define a particular Christian denomination of the Christian religion. Some use the word Catholic just make the distinction from Baptists or Methodists. While this may be how it is used on the street, the (Catholic) Church would have a more specific meaning when it uses the term catholic to define itself.

A more precise way of understanding this term in our conversation is to see the Church as universal or involving all. How amazing it was to travel to Italy and Ireland and experience the Catholic Mass.

While each spoke in their native tongue, the parts of the Mass were the same. I could follow along because I understood the flow of the Mass. Despite the fact that those people belong to different countries and cultures, we all shared the same common belief. We are all a part of the Catholic Church.

What makes us Catholic is our relationship to –Jesus, our leader and King. He established the Church and the Church derives everything from him. It is his work, through the Holy Spirit that guides and accomplishes the mission. It is his leadership, as the head of the body that will bring humanity into the divine union.

When Jesus gave the Church the mission to proclaim the Gospel to all the world (Matt. 28:16-20), he was establishing the universal characteristic of the Church. Go out to the whole world and reveal what God has done. This attribute clearly defines the nature of the Church; the Church should constantly be sharing the good news with everyone it comes in contact with.

Practical Application

Every disciple of Christ has a personal and corporate role to play in the mission of the entire Catholic Church. For years, I have encountered Catholics who profess their faith in Jesus and then declare it to be very "personal and private". This declaration has no place in the tenants of Catholicism. To be Catholic, is by its very nature, evangelistic or outgoing. While it is true that our relationship with Jesus is very personal, it cannot be so private that we don't share what we believe. Perhaps those who make this profession do so out of fear of rejection or persecution rather than living the truth of the faith?

In order to be authentic disciples who are Catholic, we have a responsibility to know what we believe and share the good news with others. Jesus didn't ask us to share the good news, he commanded us to do so. We have a responsibility to give away the amazing life-changing truth that will save souls for eternity. It is not just the work of the Clergy or religious orders but of every disciple who professes to belong to the Church. If we who profess to be children of God, will not share the great news of our Heavenly Father, then who will do it? We must grow in knowledge, then grow in faith, and ultimately give it away! Become proficient in sharing your testimony. Then engage friends and strangers with the question – Who is Jesus Christ to You? Don't forget to ask the Holy Spirit to guide you!

THE CHURCH IS APOSTOLIC

CCC 857-865

We can have tremendous confidence that the message of the Gospel and the deposit of truth remain accurate. The integrity of the Gospel remains intact because the Catholic Church, through the guidance of the Holy Spirit, has worked to pass on the unity in understanding from the eyewitnesses who were commissioned with the task of doing so. Through their effort, and those of their successors (our Bishops and Cardinals), we have an unbroken line of succession to the source of all truth - Jesus.

The Teaching Magesterium

In Matthew 28, when Jesus commissioned the Apostles with his mission, he did not give them the Bible as their source of authority. But rather, he established their apostolic office as the authority. The purpose of this office was to teach definitively in regard to what the Lord meant in his instructions to them. Some may consider this to be a faulty plan, since men have fallen from grace and their sin may certainly lead to failure. To secure the integrity of the Apostolic Office, God sent the Holy Spirit to work within the Church and it's members. Our faith lies in the work of God who planned for and enables the Teaching Magesterium to maintain the deposit of faith for all generations.

A quick glance at church history will reveal that sin is still evident in the lives of believers but the Catholic Church is the only living institution that has lasted since Christ walked the earth. Why? Because the Holy Spirit has kept it alive. In fact, if we were to go back and read the first three hundred years of the Church Father's writings, do you know what we would find? The same things we believe today.

Every church council, with the exception of Vatican II, was formed to deal with heresies (false teachings or interpretations) that had crept into the church's teachings. The Father's shepherding the Church at each time, gathered to discuss whether a popular or current thought was acceptable within the deposit of faith. A good example of one of these issues is found in Acts in the first council of Jerusalem (Acts 15).

St. Paul was having tremendous success among the Gentiles in the acceptance of the Gospel of Jesus Christ. Yet many believers in Jerusalem saw this as a threat because the "popular" thought was that a person must first convert to Judaism before they could become a Christian. This popular thought arose from a group that was very zealous in their belief. In fact, they were so zealous that they sent individuals to follow St. Paul on his missionary journeys to teach the new believers in Christ that they must first become Jewish in order for their faith in Christ to be valid.

You can imagine St. Paul's reaction. This issue became so important that a formal gathering (a council) in Jerusalem was called to discuss the question of whether a person had to become a Jew first before they could become a Christian. The deliberation was intense and extensive. St. Paul and Barnabas shared incredible testimony of what the Holy Spirit was doing among the Gentiles that ultimately made the council agree with him and St. Peter.

Since that time the deposit of truth that was given to the Church has been under assault by false religions. Efforts have been made to try to negate or water down it's meaning. It has been the work of the Bishops to keep true and pure the deposit of faith so that the Gospel of Jesus Christ can be shared to all nations for the rest of time.

The greatest threat to the Gospel is when good-hearted people start to learn about his teaching and develop their own interpretation of what the Scriptures mean. There are countless examples in church history of how individuals influenced groups of people with false teachings. It is precisely because of these destructive efforts that the Bishops have gathered to discuss teachings to determine validity within the Deposit of Truth. In their role as successors to the Apostles, the Bishops are charged with guarding what we believe and what we teach the next generations.

Practical Application

I remember going into the fifth grade and getting my math textbook. The teacher referred us to the back of the book where the answers to every third math problem were listed. The authors of the textbook had a purpose in mind. Their intention was to provide a means of helping us check our work. I remember going through the process of completing a difficult problem and flipping to the back to compare my answer. Being able to compare my answer with what was true enabled me to learn how to do the math correctly, especially when my teacher was not available.

This should become a standard for our studies of Scripture and Church Teachings. We have so many resources at our disposal for validation, to see what the Church believes about difficult situations. I wish I could tell you that every Bishop, Priest, Deacon, Religious, Catechist, Professor, Theologian and Disciple were one hundred percent accurate one hundred percent of the time but they are not.

As one who wears several of those hats, I can tell you that I do my best to be as accurate as possible but I am quite fallible. I make mistakes and misspeak periodically and, therefore, request that my audiences draw close to the Spirit and search the Church's definitive answer to any questions that may arise.

The Church has had great saints who have been wrestling with most of the same questions that people have today. They have gone through the process of exploring new thought and comparing these ideas with what the Church has defined to be true. This is where faith is required. We must have faith in the work of the Holy Spirit to lead the church in truth. Ultimately, when we use the Church's Teaching as our final word, we are trusting in the sustaining work of the Holy Spirit who seeks to keep us all in the light of truth. Spend some time examining your understanding of the faith. Look for areas where you are confused or not in agreement with the Church's teaching. Seek wise council to guide you to Church approved materials on those subjects and ask the Holy Spirit to purify your understanding of the truth.

CONCLUSION

In the training of Disciples, it is critical that we train new followers of Christ with the one truth of the Church. We have a history of people picking and choosing to believe what they want and discarding other teachings that the Church wholeheartedly embraces. Be diligent in this matter and make it your firm intention to seek the truth and live it out! Trust the Holy Spirit to provide you with a Church and believers who can guide when you are confused about specific teachings or life circumstances. If you stay close to Mother Church, you can rest knowing that you can't wander too far away from the truth that is Jesus Christ! Humility breeds openness to truth!